PRAGUE

Philippe Bénet
and
Renata Holzbachová

J·P·M
PUBLICATIONS

Contents

This Way Prague

Magical Capital

To capture some of Prague's special magic, try to observe this "Golden City" at sunrise, as it casts off its shroud of early morning mist. If you can get to the Charles Bridge before the first throngs of tourists arrive you could almost believe you were back in the Middle Ages. On both sides of the bridge loom dark, rather formidable statues of sandstone, figures from the past looking as if they have gathered here for a secret, otherworldly meeting. The sky-line is studded with domes, spires and towers, and in the background, to the northwest, Prague castle stands proudly on a hill overlooking the city.

As the sun begins to shine, and the tour groups lay claim to the city, you will discover that the old clichés are out-dated. Yesterday's dignified but fusty old lady has unhooked her corsets and has suddenly found a new lease of life as an elegant and lively socialite—the once grim, grey façades of Prague now glow with a fresh coat of pastel colours.

To restore your energy and get into the mood of the city at the same time, you might be tempted to try a typical break-fast: grilled sausage smothered in mustard, served at one of the street stands in Wenceslas Square. Or you could opt for the more subdued atmosphere of Café Evropa, a temple to Art Nouveau. In the evening, any-one who feels at home in Prague usually adjourns to a crowded, smoke-filled *pivnice* (beer cellar) for a lager or two. As they say: *Na Zdraví Praho!* To your health, Prague!

The novelist Franz Kafka warned that Prague will not let you go once you have fallen under its spell. It's difficult, indeed, not to be seduced by the charms of this bewitching city, with its dreamy, Italian atmosphere. How to define the melancholy mood that perme-ates the city? Does it come from the soft golden light shed by the street lamps, from the old cobblestones, the gracefully ornate façades, the winding alleys, the ghosts of history? It's impossible to say.

The best way to discover Prague, and to fully appreciate its colourful patchwork of archi-tectural styles, is on foot. In the Old Town, the central square with its perfect arrangement of houses looks almost unreal, like a stage set. Malá Strana (the Lesser Quarter) at the foot of the castle shows off its baroque

palaces, while Wenceslas Square flaunts its elegant Art Nouveau façades.

When night begins to fall, the "city of a hundred spires" slips back stealthily into the realms of mystery.

Bohemia and Moravia

Prague is the capital of the young Czech Republic, which has just over 10 million inhabitants. The Czechs, of Slavonic origin, are pacific and modest by nature, in the image of one of their favourite literary characters, the Good Soldier Švejk whose ingenuity always manages to triumph over the adversities of life.

While Bohemia, former playground of the Czech aristocracy, boasts a thousand castles and elegant spa towns like Marienbad, Moravia, to the east, is known for its vineyards and its lively folklore. It is carpeted with huge evergreen forests in a pleasant landscape of highlands and lakes, inhabited by enormous carp.

A crossroads of history, Prague was the glorious capital of the Holy Roman Empire during the 14th century. Bohemia and Moravia later formed part of the Habsburg empire, from

Music is ever-present in the squares of Prague.

1526 to 1918. The country was invaded by Germany during World War II, and following the war remained under communist rule until 1989.

A Society on the Move

After breaking with communism during the "Velvet Revolution", so-named because it was relatively peaceful, the young Czech Republic has eagerly embraced the market economy.

For 40 years, everything was owned by the State. Everyone had enough to live on—just about; everyone had a job, though more often than not the jobs were uninspiring and without responsibility. Franz Kafka's book *The Trial* is a good key to understanding the soul-destroying machinery of the old communist régime.

After 1989, a wave of privatization swept the land. There was a revolution in the economy, and another in the way of thinking. All the values that had been repressed for decades (such as the spirit of enterprise, a yearning for success) became indispensable in the new Czech society.

It is the young people, fresh out of university after the Velvet Revolution, who have benefited most from the change. Today, the leaders of Czech society are mostly in their thirties. For their elders, the transition has been more painful. The cost of living has risen, and retirement pensions have not kept pace. On top of it all, the old folks now have to pay for their springwater cures in the spas…

Prague itself was rejuvenated in a relatively short time. In the historical city centre, you will see that the façades have been restored to their original splendour. From 1948, when the state nationalized dwellings as well as businesses, few buildings were adequately maintained. After the fall of the totalitarian régime, many of them were returned to their former owners or their descendants, who, if they had the resources, undertook major renovation. Others were forced to sell to the real-estate speculators.

A Rich Culture

They say every Czech is born with a violin under the pillow. It may well be true. You have only to wander through the alleys of the Malá Strana quarter beneath the castle, where the city dances to the sounds of guitars, flutes and violins, joining forces with chiming clocks and tolling church bells. The Prague Spring festival, the cultural event of the year, takes place from May to June, when the walls ring with music. The wistful atmosphere of Prague has inspired a host of composers and musicians: Liszt,

Beethoven, Wagner… Mozart, fleeing Vienna, was afforded a hero's welcome here, and the première of his *Don Giovanni* was held in the Prague's Estates Theatre in 1787. While the composer Dvořák is widely known abroad, it is perhaps Smetana who best represents the Czech ideal, having devoted all his works, including eight operas, to the Czech nation.

Literary creativity flourished with the Prague-born poet Rainer Maria Rilke (1875–1926) and writer Franz Kafka, whose spirit still haunts the city which meant so much to him. Banned during the communist period, he has been reinstated as a national hero: the Czech president Václav Havel once proclaimed during an official visit: "My president is Kafka".

CZECH CHECKING

Some of the best-known Czechs are the composers Antonín Dvořák (1841–1904) and Bedřich Smetana (1824–84), artist Alfons Mucha (1860–1939), and writers Franz Kafka (1883–1924) and Milan Kundera (1929–). And also tennis champions Ivan Lendl and Martina Navrátilová; top model Eva Herzigová; film director Miloš Forman; and American Secretary of State under the Clinton administration, Madeleine Albright.

Flashback

Celts and Slavs

Several centuries before the Christian era, the Celts occupied the territories corresponding to the present-day Czech Republic. One of their tribes, the Boii, gave their name to Bohemia.

The Slavs replaced the Celts in the 6th century AD. In the 9th century Mojmir I founded the Empire of Great Moravia, which encompassed Moravia, Bohemia, Slovakia and parts of present-day Austria and Hungary. Seeking to diminish the Frankish influence in his realm, his nephew and successor Rostislav looked to the Byzantine Empire. In 863, two Byzantine missionaries, Cyril and Methodius, arrived to preach in the land of the Slavs. Part of their legacy is the Cyrillic alphabet.

The Czechs, who would eventually dominate the neighbouring Slavonic tribes, settled in Bohemia and, in 895, established their capital in Prague, under their chief Přemysl Spytihněv, founder of the Přemysl dynasty, who built the castle on the heights of the left bank of the Vltava.

Wenceslas

Prince Wenceslas, who later became the patron saint of Bohemia, spread the Christian faith in the 10th century. During his reign the St George Basilica was built in the grounds of Prague Castle.

In 950, the German emperor Otto I defeated the Czechs, and Bohemia was annexed to the Holy Roman Empire. It was not until 1212 that the Přemysl prince Otakar I recovered the throne of Bohemia as a hereditary right. Bohemia became an autonomous state.

Under Wenceslas II, who proclaimed himself King of Poland, the Czech dominions grew in size. The death of Wenceslas III, who survived his father by only a year, spelled the end of the Přemysl line, leaving the question of succession unresolved. Eventually the throne went to John of Luxembourg, son of the Holy Roman Emperor, through his marriage to Elizabeth, the daughter of Wenceslas II.

Imperial Capital

In the middle of the 14th century, under the rule of John's son Charles IV, Prague became the administrative and cultural centre of the Holy Roman Empire. Charles, who married Blanche of Valois and carried Přemysl blood through his mother's lineage, was grandson of the German emperor and

Near Prague Castle, the Strahov Monastery now houses the Museum of Literature, a veritable monument to books.

cousin of the King of France. He was an erudite ruler and a patron of the arts. He had the castle rebuilt and enticed the best architects of Europe to Prague, to embellish the city in Gothic style. The Frenchman Matthias of Arras designed St Vitus's Cathedral, while Charles Bridge and the tower at the Old Town end are the work of Peter Parler. Charles University was founded in 1348, and Prague soon become the most important city in Central Europe.

Jan Hus

The successors of Charles IV, in particular his son Wenceslas IV, were not quite up to the task of ruling the Czech kingdom. In the 14th century a Catholic priest, Jan Hus, a forerunner of Luther and Calvin, denounced the opulence of the Church and the shameless trade in Indulgences. In 1402, he became the preacher at the Bethlehem Chapel in Prague, then in 1409, rector of the Charles University. His ideas earned him excommunication from the Church in 1412. Having faith and trust in Wenceslas IV, who promised him protection, he went to the Council of Constance two years later to defend his ideas. Refusing to renounce them, he was taken prisoner and burned at the stake in Constance in 1415.

This execution sparked a revolution which was to mark the country's history profoundly. Today, Jan Hus remains a national hero: the anniversary of his death has become a holiday and the Czech clergy has been campaigning (unsuccessfully, so far) for his canonization.

The Habsburgs

In the musical chairs of royal marriages and successions, the crown of Bohemia fell to the Habsburgs in 1526. Vienna was preferred to Prague as their capital, Catholicism was imposed on the Czech people and the Renaissance style on their architecture. Under Rudolf II (1576–1611), who surrounded himself with a glittering court, Prague once again became the capital of the Empire.

The Protestant Czech nobility had significant differences with the House of Austria, and matters came to a head when, on May 23, 1618, representatives of the Protestant estates hurled two imperial governors out the window of the Castle chancellery. The "Defenestration of Prague" (in fact this was not the first time this expedient method was used to settle disputes) sparked the Thirty Years' War. The estates of Bohemia were ultimately defeated in the Battle of the White Mountain. Numerous executions followed in the Old Town Square, and Bohemia lost its autonomy. Part of the Czech nobility was exiled.

An underground movement to revive the Czech national identity was set up around 1780, as intellectuals became dedicated to the defence of the Czech language and literature. In 1868, the construction of the National Theatre, built thanks to donations from all over the country, symbolized the Czech people's new-found pride. Czech architecture and music enjoyed a revival.

Thanks to strong economic development at the beginning of the 20th century, Bohemia became the industrial hub of Austria-Hungary, and factories such as Škoda hummed with activity.

Independence

After World War I, the first Republic of Czechoslovakia was proclaimed on October 28, 1918 by Tomáš G. Masaryk. The territories of Bohemia, Moravia, and Slovakia were thus united, and the Czech people could at last enjoy an uncensored press, freedom of expression and other benefits of democracy. The economy continued to prosper and culture flourished during the 1920s, when Czechoslovakia was as highly developed as

Great Britain. There remained the problem of disenchanted German, Hungarian, Polish and Ukrainian minorities. The good times didn't last long, for war was brewing over the border.

Hitler laid claim to the Sudetenland, in Bohemia, which had a strong German community. Let down by France and Great Britain at the Conference of Munich in 1938 (in spite of past treaties of intervention in case of conflict), the Czech president Beneš had no other resort but to cede the disputed territory. The German army invaded the country.

Prague was liberated by the Soviets on May 9, 1945, and more than $3^1/2$ million Germans were expelled. The Czechs, remembering the 1938 betrayal by the French and British, turned to the Soviets; in the 1946 elections the Communist Party obtained 40% of the vote. Industry and commerce were nationalized and freedom of expression was abolished. Many fled the country. Those who stayed at home witnessed the purges and trials of the Stalin era in the 1950s. The country acquired a new, unequivocal name in 1960: the Socialist Republic of Czechoslovakia.

In 1968, the winds of freedom blowing across Europe were felt in the east. Supported by a population eager for change, the new secretary general of the Communist Party, Alexander Dubček, advocated a "Socialism with a human face". It was the flowering of the Prague Spring. In response, on August 21, 1968, Soviet troops invaded the country to ensure its "normalization". Dissidence continued throughout the 1970s, leading to the birth of the Charter 77 group, formed by intellectuals opposed to the regime.

The Velvet Revolution

In 1989, the fall of the Berlin Wall unleashed a tidal wave of hope throughout Eastern Europe. A student demonstration inspired by the Civic Forum, a dissident movement, gathered 30,000 people in Prague to acclaim Václav Havel, an intellectual who had spent several years behind bars.

Václav Havel was elected president of the Republic on December 30, 1989, the culmination of the Velvet Revolution. On January 1, 1993, Czechoslovakia split into Slovakia and the Czech Republic.

Under prime minister Václav Klaus the Czech Republic swung towards liberalism, but the people voted against him in 1997. As the new millennium dawns, the country's economy is beginning to prosper and the Czechs are looking forward to joining the EU.

On the Scene

The best way to explore the historical centre is on foot, observing the city's amazing mixture of architectural styles—Romanesque, Gothic, Renaissance, classical, baroque, Art Nouveau, cubist. When looking for an address, bear in mind that the words for "street" or "avenue" are never indicated on signs. Thus Národní 14 means 14, Národní Street. On the other hand, the word for square, *náměstí* (abbr. *nám.*) is frequently used. Václavske náměstí 14 is 14, Wenceslas Square.

WALKS

Prague is made up of four towns which were united administratively in 1784: on the left bank of the river, dominating the town, is Hradčany, the castle district and, at its feet along the river front, Malá Strana, the Lesser Quarter. On the opposite bank are Staré Město, the Old Town, and Nové Město, the New Town. Our walking tour starts in the New Town, on Wenceslas Square. Follow Na Příkopě Street, then Celetná to reach the Old Town Square. A maze of crooked streets and alleyways surrounds this square, without doubt the most attractive in Prague. Next, heading along Karlová, you arrive at the famous Charles Bridge.

On the other side of the river, you should take time to explore Malá Strana, a peaceful quarter of baroque palaces, stately embassies and elegant gardens. Finally, climb the hill to the imposing castle and its surroundings, from where there are remarkable views over the city.

NOVÉ MĚSTO

Planned from the 14th century, the New Town was fully renovated in the 19th and 20th centuries.

Wenceslas Square

⋮ Václavské náměstí
⋮ Metro Můstek or Muzeum

Founded in the 14th century and largely remodelled in the 20th, this is the commercial and banking centre of the Czech capital. The oblong space is guarded by the bronze equestrian figure of Prince Wenceslas, surrounded by the statues of four Bohemian saints. The square has witnessed several significant historical events: the 1918 demonstrations that led to the establishment of an independent state; the self-sacrifice of the young Czech student Jan Palach, who burned himself to death in 1969 in protest against the Soviet presence; the moving speech by Václav Havel in 1989 that ushered in a new era.

The National Museum dominating the scene with its golden dome is on the other side of a busy thoroughfare, built contrary to all common sense during the communist regime.

At the opposite end of the square, at no. 1, is the Koruna Palace. At no. 34, the Wiehl house boasts a neo-Renaissance façade.

To the right, Na Příkopě borders the Old Town. On the left, you reach National Street and the National Theatre.

National Museum

⋮ Národní muzeum
⋮ Metro Muzeum
⋮ Open daily 9 a.m.–5 p.m.
⋮ Closed first Tuesday of the month

Flaunting a somewhat intimidating neo-Renaissance façade, this imposing building houses a monumental stairway which leads to the Pantheon. Here the country's history is illustrated by a series of busts and statues of famous men. There are also interesting collections of minerals, prehistoric objects, zoology and palaeontology.

Hotel Evropa

⋮ Václavské náměstí 25
⋮ Café open 7 a.m.–midnight
⋮ Tel. 242 281 17; fax 242 245 44

The Hotel Evropa is a monument to Art Nouveau, a style inspired by baroque which flourished between 1897 and 1910. The hotel's famous façade is adorned with gilded lettering and floral motifs, mosaics, and wrought-iron balconies. If the hotel has a somewhat faded charm, the café on the ground floor will take you back to the carefree atmosphere of the early 20th century. Peep into the restaurant to view Art Nouveau style in all its splendour: wrought-iron banisters, mahogany woodwork, stained glass, gilded bronze caryatids…

Church of Our Lady of the Snows

Chrám Panny Marie Sněžné
Jungmannovo náměstí
Heading down from Wenceslas Square, turn left on 28. října Street, to reach Jungmannovo Square.

HISTORY IN STONE

Romanesque art made its appearance in Bohemia in the 11th century. Prague acquired three Romanesque rotundas, and the St George basilica in the castle grounds.

The Gothic style spread under the reign of the Emperor Charles IV (1346–78). Typical is St Vitus's Cathedral, light and airy. It was begun by the Frenchman Matthias of Arras and completed by the German Peter Parler. Other examples of Gothic architecture: the Old-New Synagogue on Červená Street; Charles Bridge and its towers; the Powder Gate; the Church of Our Lady of Týn (Old Town Square).

Under Emperor Rudolf II (1576–1611), the Renaissance style flourished in Prague. The Italian influence is plainly visible in the trompe-l'œil effect of many buildings and the use of the sgraffito ("scratched") technique to decorate the façades. Examples are Prague Castle (the old royal palace), Schwarzenberg Palace, 7, Hradčanské Square; House of the Minute in the Old Town Square.

Under the Habsburgs and the House of Austria, Catholicism was imposed as the state religion. The baroque style (17th–18th centuries), often heavy and over-ornate, blossomed here in St Nicholas's Cathedral in the Lesser Quarter, with voluptuous concave and convex curves, expressive statues and a profusion of stucco. The intention was to inspire a feeling of awe. Other examples: Valdštejn Palace and the Church of Our Lady of Loreto.

In the second half of the 18th century, the exuberance of baroque was taken even further with the rococo style favoured by Empress Maria Theresa. This is illustrated by the Goltz-Kinský Palace on the Old Town Square.

Erected in 1347, this church was "baroquified" in the 18th century. The main altar is the largest in Prague. The gardens, bordering a former Franciscan convent, are a haven of peace within the New Town.

National Avenue
⋮ Národní

The National Avenue leads you to the river. Look up at the gilded Art Nouveau architecture of the former Prague Savings Bank at no. 7 and on the façade of the Topič house, no. 9.

National Theatre
⋮ Národní divadlo
⋮ Národní 2

Built between 1868 and 1881, this neo-Renaissance building dominates the Masaryk riverside quays. It is striking, both inside and out, and was rebuilt thanks to private donations following a fire at the end of the 19th century. The National Theatre symbolizes Czech national identity and pride.

Na Příkopě

At the northern end of Wenceslas Square, turn right along Na Příkopě, full of banks. At no. 10, note the Sylva-Taroucca Palace which today houses the casino; at no. 14, the 19th-century Church of the Holy Cross; at no. 20, the Živnostenská Banka, which occupies a neo-Renaissance palace. At no. 22 stands the Slavonic House, originally baroque and later remodelled in the classical style.

Mucha Museum
⋮ Kaunický palác
⋮ Panská 7
⋮ Open daily 10 a.m.–6 p.m.

Recently opened, this museum displays more than 80 works by the painter and decorator Alfons Mucha: paintings, photographs, charcoal sketches, pastels and lithographs, in addition to personal items. Born in Moravia in 1860, Mucha started out as a stage-set decorator. He went to study in Munich, then moved on to Paris, where he eventually acquired fame and fortune. At first he made his living as illustrator for the newspaper, *La Vie parisienne*. In 1894 the French actress Sarah Bernhardt chose one of his innovative designs for a poster, and from then onwards, he never looked back. Mucha is famous for his sensual paintings of willowy women with long, loose locks of hair. After a disappointing trip to New York, Mucha returned to Prague in 1910, where he completed a well-known series of twenty paintings portraying Czech mythological and historical themes. He also decorated the

Among the treasures in the Mucha Museum is this 1911 poster of Princezna Hyacinta (detail).

Municipal House and designed the stained-glass windows in St Vitus's Cathedral.

After the Velvet Revolution, Mucha's grandson decided to gather together his works, creating the Alfons Mucha Foundation in 1992.

Municipal House
⋮ Obecní dům
⋮ Náměstí Republiky

At the end of Na Příkopě, you reach Republic Square, site of this splendid building in the purest Art Nouveau style. This outstanding monument, its exterior somewhat reminiscent of a cruise liner, has been entirely restored. Notice the floral motifs, the stucco, the use of wrought iron. The colourful semicircular pediment is adorned with an exquisite mosaic, *A homage to Prague*.

The Municipal House was built as a cultural centre at the beginning of the 20th century, on the site of the former royal palace, which had burned down. Fashionable sculptors including Václav Myslbek, and painters such as Alfons Mucha and Max Švabinský took part in its design. Although the Mucha Hall is not normally open to the public, the Smetana Hall with its ceiling

painted by František Ženíšek is used for concerts. Recently renovated, the building now houses two restaurants, the Francouzská (French) Restaurace and Plzeňská Restaurace in the basement.
The Kavárna Café (entrance from no. 10, Národni) was known as a meeting place for intellectuals. It's a good address for a casual drink.

Powder Gate

- Prašná Brána
- Open 10 a.m.–6 p.m.
- April 1 to November 2.
- Admission fee.

A small stone stairway leads to the top of the gate's tower, from where you have a view over the entire Old Town. The tower was a gunpowder store during the 18th century. You have to pass beneath it to reach the Old Town, by Celetná Street.
This marks the beginning of the Royal Way, the route followed by the kings during their coronation ceremony.

STARÉ MĚSTO

On the right bank of the river, the Old Town developed in a bend of the river during the 10th century. It has

---

ART NOUVEAU

At the end of the 19th century, a movement of artistic renewal swept across Europe. It produced the Secession Movement in Vienna, Jugendstil in Germany and Art Nouveau in Prague. This last spread through Bohemia between 1897 and 1910, drawing on Czech baroque. Sharp angles disappeared as lines became slender and fluid, inspired by nature—lilies, leaves and tendrils. Steel, glass, iron and wood was worked to resemble insects, flowers and vegetation.

The Hotel Evropa counts among the jewels of Art Nouveau. In the café and the hotel dining room, much use has been made of mahogany and stained glass. The stair banisters are made of wrought iron. Near the Powder Gate, the Municipal House is another fine example of the same style, with a striking façade. Numerous artists contributed to the building, including Alfons Mucha, who became very popular in Paris at the end of the 19th century. He invented an elongated shape for theatre posters (notably for actress Sarah Bernhardt) and designed numerous advertisements in which everything from biscuits to bicycles were illustrated by slender female figures.

Other examples of Art Nouveau style in Prague are the Masaryk quays near the National Theatre, and the main railway station, east of Wenceslas Square.

retained its medieval air and timeless charm.

Celetná Street

Lined by Gothic houses with added baroque touches, Celetná is one of the oldest streets in Prague. The façades of nos. 36, 23 and 21 are particularly handsome. At no. 34, the House of the Black Madonna is considered a model of cubist architecture. The pediment of the building at no. 22 is adorned with gilded letters in French which means: "Jewellers by appointment of His Majesty". At no. 12, under the porch of the baroque Hrzán Palace, you can wander into Hrzánská passageway. See the magnificent Sixt House at no. 2, with its busts of emperors.

Old Town Square

⋮ Staroměstské náměstí

Celetná Street takes you to the most beautiful square in Prague, which in the Middle Ages was a marketplace and where duels were fought.

It looks slightly unreal, like a theatre set, with its colourful cut-out façades and red tile roofs. All kinds of styles are represented: Gothic porches, Renaissance frescoes, baroque pediments…

The Old Town Square is overlooked by the belfry of the Town Hall to the west, and the turreted towers of

Our Lady of Týn church to the east. In the centre of the square stands the memorial to Jan Hus, the Catholic priest who spoke out against the extravagance of the Church in the 14th century, and who became a national hero after being burned at the stake.

Have your camera ready to capture the exquisite façades: that of the Štorch House at no. 16 (late-19th century) can be recognized from the fresco depicting St Wenceslas as a triumphant knight. At no. 17, see the House of the Stone Ram, whose portal dates from the 16th century, and the 14th-century House of the Stone Table.

To the left of the Týn church, at no. 12, stands the Goltz-Kinský palace, perhaps the finest example of rococo style. Count Goltz commissioned it from the Italian architect Anselmo Lurago in the 18th century. Next door to the Goltz palace, the House of the Stone Bell dates from the 14th century. Don't miss the lovely façade of the building at no. 6.

Czech Glass Museum

⋮ Staroměstské náměstí 26
⋮ Open 10 a.m.–7.30 p.m.
⋮ Tel. 24 23 80 51.

Interesting museum of glass and crystal, displaying fine pieces from the 13th to 20th centuries. The entire history of glass-making is documented, from medieval times, when beads were incorporated into the design, through Renaissance (painted hunting and religious scenes), baroque crystal (incredibly transparent, finely engraved), to splendid table services of the 1930s. Make sure you have time to watch the skilled glassblowers at work, at the end of your tour.

Our Lady of Týn

- U Matky Boží Před Týnem
- Staroměstské náměstí 14

Pass under the arches of the Týn School (built from the 14th–16th centuries) and the 18th-century House of the White Unicorn to reach Our Lady of Týn, built on the site of a former 10th-century church belonging to a hospice reserved for traders. Týn was a Hussite church, but since the Counter-Reformation it became a Catholic bastion, and a baroque décor soon crept in. Of particular interest are the paintings by Karel Škréta, the high altar, and the altars of St Barbara and St Joseph.

Courtyard of the Traders of Týn

The Tynská alley which runs alongside Our Lady of Týn wanders through a maze of alleyways and courtyards. The façades of the apartments buildings were recently, and attractively, restored. The merchants traded in the the Týn courtyard up to the 18th century.

Estates Theatre

- Stavovské divadlo
- Železná 11

Železná Street starts at the Old Town Square, passing alongside the imposing Carolinum building (the administrative centre for the Charles University), to end at the Estates Theatre, also known by its former name, Týl Theatre. It was built between 1781 and 1783 in the classical style. The first performance of Mozart's *Don Giovanni* was staged here in 1787.

Old Town Hall

- Staroměstská Radnice
- Staroměstské náměstí 1
- Guided tour (35 min) in English, 9 a.m.–5.30 p.m. in summer, 9 a.m.–5 p.m. in winter.
- Tower (admission fee) open 9 a.m.–5.30 p.m.

The Old Town Hall was founded in 1338, and developed through the centuries to match the city's growth in size and importance. Its most obvious highlight is the astronomical clock. The Old Town Hall is made up of several buildings, including the House of the Minute, with 17th-century sgraffito decorations. The Kříž House has a beautiful Renaissance window and a baroque grid with the inscription: Praga Caput Regni (Prague, capital of the realm). Also note the series of 15th-century coats of arms on the façade.

The guided tour takes in the lobby, the 14th-century Council Chamber and the Session Hall. It's well worth paying the small fee to visit the top of the tower: the view over the rooftops of the Old Town and of the castle hill is superb.

Astronomical Clock
: Staroměstské náměstí

Dating from 1410 and modified in the 16th century, the astronomical clock consisting of two circular faces is the most curious sight in the square. The upper dial represents the Earth, in the centre, with the planets orbiting around it. The face below, showing the months and the signs of the zodiac, dates from the 19th century. Above the two is a mechanism activating various characters and symbolic objects which burst into activity every hour. Christ and the Apostles appear, then vanish. A gong sounds, and Death brandishes its scythe, tolls the knell and turns over the hour glass. then it's the turn of Greed to show his purse, and Vanity admires himself in a mirror. A Turkish prince shakes his head to indicate that he doesn't yet want to abandon combat, an allusion to the Turkish invasion of Central Europe in the 16th and 17th centuries. Then a cock spreads its wings and crows in a raucous finale.

St Nicholas Cathedral
: Chrám svatého Mikuláše
: Staroměstské náměstí
: Open Tuesday–Friday
: 10 a.m.– noon, and
: Wednesday 2–4 p.m.

The Cathedral of St Nicholas is located at the corner of Pařížská (Paris Street). The interior is especially fine, with its galleries and arcades, not to mention the sublime fresco in the dome. German merchants built a Gothic church on the site in the 13th century. Today, St Nicholas is a Hussite church.

Pařížská
Leading off Old Town Square, Paris Street is lined with lavish turn-of-the-century buildings which replaced the small houses in the Jewish quarter, at one time enclosed within a ghetto.

JOSEFOV
Arriving in Prague in the 10th century, the Jewish traders were gathered into a single quarter. Their rights were recognized by the Emperor of

Austria Joseph II (1780–90), and thus the Jewish Quarter became known as Josefov, in his honour. But the Jews did not obtain equal rights until 1867. Apart from a few well-to-do money lenders, most were poor and lived a cramped existence in the ghetto. The maze of winding alleys and tiny houses was finally razed in 1892.

Jewish Museum

- Židovské Muzeum
- Maisel, Pinkas and Klaus synagogues. Guided tours (2 hr) from the Maisel synagogue.

GOLEM

Every Czech, young and old alike, is familiar with the legend of the Golem, an imaginary character whose mission was to defend the Jewish community. The legend goes that Christians were becoming hostile towards the Jews, believing they made human sacrifices during their religious festivals. To protect the Jews from reprisals, Rabbi Löw fashioned out of clay a being with superhuman powers, the Golem, which obeyed him. But one day the rabbi forgot to give the Golem its instructions, and the vengeful creature went on a destructive rampage. Löw was obliged to remove the Golem's magical powers, and it turned back to clay.

- Open Sunday to Friday
- 9 a.m.– 5.30 p.m.

The Jewish museum was created in 1906. In 1942, the Nazis decided to assemble the works of art and religious objects left by the 153 Jewish communities in the Czech country, many of whom had been deported. The museum became the property of the state under the communists and it wasn't until 1994 that the Jews recovered their possessions. This museum, which today has one of the world's largest collections of Jewish art with more than 40,000 objects and 10,000 books, is housed in three synagogues. The entry ticket also gives access to the old cemetery and the Old-New Synagogue, the oldest in Europe, still used as a place of worship.

Maisel Synagogue

- Maiselova synagoga
- Maiselova 10

Reconstructed in neo-Gothic style on the site of a 16th-century synagogue, it contains an impressive collection of gold, silver and pewter objects used in Jewish ceremonies.

Pinkas Synagogue

- Pinkasova synagoga
- Široká 3

This synagogue is at the bottom of the old Jewish cemetery. The foundations date from the 11th century and were modified in 1625. The walls were chosen as a memorial in honour of the victims of the Holocaust, whose names are inscribed here. Do not miss the heart-wrenching exhibition of drawings made by children in the Terezín deportation camp, supposedly a model camp.

Old Jewish Cemetery

- Starý židovský Hřbitov
- Entrance through the Pinas Synagogue, Široká 3

A forest of Gothic, Renaissance and classical gravestones are planted in the ground, seeming to struggle for space. The oldest tomb is that of the poet Abigdor Karo, who died on April 25, 1439. From the 15th century up to 1787, graves were laid on top of each other in this cemetery, sometimes reaching twelve superimposed layers. It has been estimated that this is the final resting place for some 200,000 people. On certain stones, carved images refer to the trade of the occupant; a mortar, for example, indicates a pharmacist.

Klaus Synagogue

- Klausova synagoga
- U starého hřbitova 1

Exposition of objects related to Jewish customs and traditions

Old-New Synagogue

- Staronová synagoga
- Červená

This is the oldest vestige of the Jewish quarter, and the oldest synagogue in Europe. When it was built in the 13th century, the Gothic construction was called simply the "new synagogue". Its small size gives a good idea of the tiny dimensions of the other houses in the ghetto. It is still used as a place of worship.

The hall is covered with a 6-ribbed vault supported by two octagonal pillars. Notice the porch (the oldest element of the building), the 16th- and 18th-century wrought-iron chandeliers, and the grid around the cantor's platform which dates from the 15th century.

Jewish Town Hall

- Židovská radnice
- Maiselova18

Next to the Old-New Synagogue, at the top of a house built in the 16th century and refurbished in the 18th, you can see a clock with Hebrew figures whose hands turn anti-clockwise (Hebrew is read from right to left).

TO CHARLES BRIDGE

For nearly four centuries the Charles Bridge, built in the 14th century, was the only way across the Vtlava river.

Lesser Square

From the Old Town Square, pass in front of the Astronomical Clock and the Old Town Hall to reach Malé náměstí, lined with attractive Renaissance and Gothic façades. The well in the centre of this square, closed by an elegant wrought-iron grid, dates from 1560. At no. 11, take the gallery that leads into a network of winding streets boasting freshly renovated façades. Recently restored, the pharmacy U Zlaté Koruny, at no. 13, was built in 1887. The interior is superbly decorated in dark wood. At no. 3, the Rott House, restored in 1996, is adorned with neo-Renaissance frescoes by Mikoláš Aleš. It now houses a luxury food store which is well worth a visit. In the wine cellar you can admire Romanesque remains and bottles of first-class vintages from all over the world.

Karlova and Husova streets

Narrow Karlova Street, usually thronged with tourists, threads its way to Charles Bridge. At no. 8, note the stone porch of the Unitaria Palace. An inscription on no. 4 states that Johannes Kepler, the famous alchemist to Rudolf II, once lived here. Turn off into Husova Street (less crowded), intersecting Karlova. The imposing porch at no. 20 is flanked by a pair of gigantic Atlas statues. This is the Clam-Gallas Palace, housing the city archives. Note the attractive fresco on no. 15, representing a couple of wine-makers holding a bunch of grapes. And don't miss the tavern U Zlatého Tygra at no. 17, a typical noisy, smoky watering hole.

Bethlehem Chapel

- Betlémská Kaple
- Betlémské náměstí
- Open daily 9 a.m.–6 p.m. April–October; 9 a.m.–5 p.m. November–March.

A short detour along Husova, to the left, takes you to the Bethlehem Chapel, rebuilt in 1950 according to ancient manuscripts and the original plans. Jan Hus preached here in 1402.

St Giles's Church

- Kostel Svatého Jiljí
- Husova 8

Built in the 14th century, this Gothic church was a Hussite parish before it passed on to the Dominicans in the 17th century. The interior was "baroquified" in the 18th century. Observe the pilasters and pillars, and the ceiling frescoes. At one time the church was patronized by French merchants, and some of the altars have inscriptions in French.

Endless comings and goings on the twelve bridges that link the two banks of the Vltava river.

Knights of the Cross Square

⋮ Křižovnické náměstí

Continuing along Karlova you reach the river, Charles Bridge and the Knights of the Cross Square.
On the right, the baroque church of St Clement (Svatého Klimenta, Karlova 1) was part of a group of imposing buildings called the Clementinum, which today houses the State Library. The Jesuits undertook construction of this complex in the middle of the 17th century; it comprises a college, two churches and two chapels. Look out for the tramways when you cross the road! To your right, the Church

of St Francis (Kostel Sv. Františka) features sublime ceilings and a superb baroque organ, dating from 1702. The concerts held in the church are outstanding. In front of the church, a massive statue of Charles IV beckons you to discover the bridge bearing his name.

CHARLES BRIDGE AND THE RIVER BANKS

As you cross the Charles Bridge, built in the 14th and 15th centuries, a wonderfully romantic view unfolds on either side of the river. On the left bank, the castle towers over the city. Below it the baroque palaces of Malá

Strana, the Lesser Quarter, huddled at one end of the bridge, are capped by red-tiled roofs: a genuinely medieval setting, unique in Europe.

If you don't like crowds, get up early and see the bridge at dawn, when you can have it all to yourself.

Charles Bridge

Karlův most
Tower open 10 a.m.–6.30 p.m. in summer, 10 a.m.–5 p.m. in winter. Admission fee.

Two dark, crenellated towers rise on either side of the bridge. On the right bank, the Old Town side of the river, the first of the towers (Mostecká Věž), was designed by Peter Parler in the 15th century. A narrow stone stairway leads to the top, offering an interesting view of the bridge and castle. On one side of the tower you can see the sculpted heads of Wenceslas IV, St Vitus and the Emperor Charles IV. Constructed of dark sandstone blocks, the bridge measures 520 m (1,700 ft) in length and is 9.5 m (31 ft) wide. Its entire length is adorned with thirty statues added in the 18th and 19th centuries, though most of those you see today are copies of the originals (see pp. 60–61).

The bridge used to link two independent townships, Malá Strana and Staré Město. Charles IV commissioned the architect Peter Parler to replace the old Judith Bridge, which stood on the same site and had been swept away by floods. Work started in 1357. Recent analysis has revealed that eggs, milk and wine were added to the mortar as a binding agent.

A strange punishment was enacted in front of the third statue to the left, representing a Pietà: it's said that bakers caught skimping on the flour would be locked in a cage and lowered into the freezing waters of the Vltava.

In the middle of the bridge is the only bronze statue, and also the oldest, which portrays St John Nepomuk. The saint is shown holding a crucifix, and around his head is a halo and stars. A plaque indicates the place where Jan Nepomucký, the cathedral vicar, was thrown into the Vltava in 1393, tied up in a sack. Apparently, he was executed because, as confessor to the Queen, he was privy to unspeakable confidences. Today, statues of St John Nepomuk adorn numerous bridges both in the Czech Republic and in Austria. He was retrieved from obscurity in the 17th century by the Jesuits, who needed a local Catholic saint to help forget the reformist zeal of Jan Hus. They chose a man of the same Christian name who was, like

Hus, put to death to be kept quiet. Close to the Malá Strana end of the bridge, you'll see the statue of the knight Bruncvík carrying a sword and a coat of arms showing a lion, the symbol of his courage. The citizens of the Old Town erected the statue in 1506, in full view of the burghers of Malá Strana, just to show them to whom the bridge and the river really belonged. On top of that they exacted a toll from those crossing the bridge.

The towers at the end of the bridge count among the oldest vestiges in Prague. The left-hand tower was part of the old 12th-century Judith Bridge; that on the right was added in 1464. Its gable ends and ornamentation date from 1591. Down on the right, you can see one of the oldest hotels in Prague: U Tří Pštrosů (The House of the Three Ostriches) which was built during Charles IV's reign.

The Vltava

Eleven bridges link the two banks of the Vltava, which the composer Smetana immortalized in a symphony (outside the Czech Republic, it is best known by its German name: Moldau).

The Old Town nestles on the left bank, dominated by the resplendent neo-Renaissance National Theatre. It was built between 1868 and 1881 and funded by popular subscription. Further on, the Masaryk quayside boasts several superb Art Nouveau façades (such as the Goethe Institute).

MALÁ STRANA

The Lesser Quarter must be one of the most pleasant districts in Prague for a quiet stroll. Here you'll find the foreign embassies, baroque palaces, peaceful gardens and outdoor restaurants overlooking the Vltava.

Otakar II founded the Lesser Quarter in 1257 and invited German merchants to settle here. Charles IV later enlarged the district. When Rudolf II of Habsburg (1576–1611) made Prague his capital, he surrounded himself with a glamorous court and invited renowned Italian architects. The nobility and merchants built palaces at the foot of the castle.

Kampa is a romantic area below Charles Bridge. If you follow Mostecká Street and then, to the left, Lázeňská Street, you reach Malta Square (Maltézské náměstí), home of the Japanese Embassy, and the Turba and Nostic palaces (the latter houses the Dutch Embassy).

Our Lady Beneath the Chain

⋮ Kostel Panny Marie Pod Řetězem Dating from the 12th century, this is the oldest church in Malá Strana, standing on the site of a Romanesque basilica. It belonged to the Knights of Malta.

Velkopřevorské Square

⋮ Velkopřevorské náměstí

This tree-shaded square at the end of Lázeňská Street is bordered by the Hrzán Palace (no. 1) with its Renaissance portal, the Buquoy Palace (no. 2), home of the French Embassy, and the Palace of the Grand Prior of the Order of Malta (no. 4).

At the far end of the square, a small bridge crosses an arm of the Vltava. On the left is a water mill known, for some obscure reason, as the Devil's Mill. You will not realise it, but Kampa is in fact an island. Its enchanting atmosphere attracts romantics from all over the world.

If you take Hroznová Street on the right, then Na Kampě, you will discover the lawns of a large park where all the young Czechs come to sunbathe in summer.

You can head back along the riverside to pass under the Charles Bridge and roam further down the banks.

Our Lady of Victory

⋮ Kostel Panny Marie Vítězné
⋮ Karmelitská 9
⋮ Open from 8 a.m.–2 p.m.

Very popular with Italian and Spanish tourists, this church is famous for a small wax figure known as the Holy Infant of Prague, brought from Spain more than 300 years ago. It is 46 cm (18 in) high, with a crown of gold encrusted with precious stones, and is the object of special reverence in a number of countries.

The church acquired its baroque ornamentation from the Spanish Carmelites. Note on many altars paintings in the style of Petr Brandl (1700).

Lesser Quarter Square

⋮ Malostranské náměstí

Heading west along Mostecká Street, you reach the largest square in the Malá Strana quarter, encircling a group of apartment buildings and St Nicholas Cathedral, with an impressive dome and spire.

At no. 21, the former Malá Strana town hall (Malostranská Beseda) now houses, on the first floor, a trendy café and a jazz club popular with young people. The Renaissance house U Splavínů, remodelled in the baroque style in 1720, features a fresco portraying the coronation of the Virgin Mary. Other buildings of great beauty include no. 25, the Kaiserštejn House, dating from the 18th century, and no. 19, the entrance to the Czech National Assembly (along Tomášská Street).

At the upper end of the square, the Liechtenstein Palace (no. 13) is well known to musicians as the headquarters of the Academy of Music. The column in the centre of the square was erected in 1715.

St Nicholas Cathedral

- Chrám svatého Mikuláše
- Malostranské náměstí
- Open daily 9 a.m.–5 p.m. April–October and 9 a.m.–4 p.m. November–March.

This cathedral is one of the finest examples of baroque style in Prague. It is the work of the architect Kryštof Dientzenhofer and his son Kilián Ignác Dientzenhofer. Construction began in 1673 on the site of an old Gothic church. Inside, look up at the ceiling, covered with an immense fresco illustrating the life of St Nicholas. Behind the organ, another fresco documents the life of St Cecilia. The fresco in the dome represents the Holy Trinity. The pulpit, from 1765, is particularly handsome.

Wallenstein Gardens

- Valdštejnská zahrada
- Entrance at Letenská 10
- Open daily from 8 a.m.–7 p.m. from May to September.

Wallenstein Palace (Valdštejnský palác) is another remarkable example of baroque construction, designed by Italian architects between 1623 and 1630. It is not open to visitors, but you can wander around the gardens, picturesquely laid out with statues (copies of the originals by Adrien de Vries), fountains and geometrical flower beds. It makes the perfect setting for a rest before you climb up to the castle.

In summer, concerts and plays are staged here in the cool of the evening.

Ledebourg and Palffy Gardens

- Entrance: Valdštejnské náměstí 3
- Open daily 10 a.m.–6 p.m.
- January to October

Here you may well think you are in Tuscany. These terraced gardens, laid out in the 18th century and recently restored, provide an alternative route to the castle, avoiding the streets.

Concerts and plays are organized here in summer. These elegant, tranquil gardens are one of Prague's little secrets.

Nerudova Street

This is the main road to the castle. Starting at Lesser Quarter Square, the steep street bears the name of a

Czech writer who lived in the House of the Two Suns, no. 47, and the House of the Three Black Eagles, no. 44.

The striking building at no. 5 is the Morzin Palace, now housing the Romanian embassy; while that at no. 20, built 1721–26 by an Italian architect, is the Italian embassy. Some of the apartment buildings have lovely frescoes, but you have to look up to see them: the House of the Three Fiddles, no 12, and the House of the Red Ram, no. 11.

HRADČANY

Northwest of the Vtlava, looming over the city, the Castle district has been considered a separate town since the 9th century. It spreads over 45 ha (112 acres), encompassing the cathedral and its two spires, a basilica, three courtyards, several streets and alleys, and a number of noteworthy monuments and museums. The castle, the former royal residence, is today the home of the President of the Republic. Its construction retraces the country's history over the centuries from the origins of the Czech nation in 870.

The Castle

Hradčanské náměstí
Castle esplanade open daily
5 a.m.–midnight April–October;
6 a.m.–11 p.m. November–March.

Changing of the Guard at the castle gates every hour on the hour, 5 a.m.–11 p.m., with fanfare and changing of the flag at noon.
Castle buildings open daily 9 a.m.–5 p.m. April–October, 9 a.m.–4 p.m. November–March. Closed December 24.
Information service in Third Courtyard, or tel. 243 733 68; fax 243 108 96. Three-day entry pass available. Audio tape tour and Braille guide.

First Courtyard

The castle entrance is guarded by two awe-inspiring statues of giants engaged in combat, with dagger and bludgeon to despatch their enemies. Emblazoned on the gate's grid is the monogram of Maria Theresa, Empress of Austria. The ceremony of the Changing of the Guard (resplendent in uniforms redesigned by Theodor Pisek, responsible for the costumes in *Amadeus*) is a sight not to be missed. The buildings around this courtyard (1760) are by Niccolo Pacassi. Pass under the Matthias Gate to reach the second courtyard.

Second Courtyard

The buildings and façades of this courtyard, originally 16th century,

It could be a country village, but in fact it is Cernínská Street, in the castle district.

were modified by Pacassi during the reign of Maria Theresa in the 18th century. To the right, you reach the Chapel of the Holy Cross, built between 1756 and 1763 and containing objects from the cathedral treasury.

In the centre of the square stands a baroque sandstone fountain. The buildings to the left, the former stables of Ferdinand I and Rudolf II, now house the Castle Gallery. This magnificent collection of Renaissance and baroque paintings includes prestigious works of many old masters, among them Titian and Rubens.

Concerts are held in the exquisite Spanish Hall on the first floor.

If you take the passageway which leads outside the castle, you will see, on the left, a baroque building that once housed a riding school. To the right is the the Powder Tower where Rudolf II's alchemists conducted their experiments, and further away, the elegant Belvedere pavilion, built in the purest Renaissance style.

Come back to the Second Courtyard. Under the porch giving access to the Third Courtyard and the cathedral, a staircase leads to the offices of the Czech President.

St Vitus's Cathedral
⋮ Katedrála Sv. Víta

You have to look up to appreciate this massive cathedral, which fills most of the courtyard. Emperor Charles IV commissioned the French architect Matthias of Arras to start its construction in 1344, on the site of a Romanesque rotunda and basilica. The work was continued by Peter Parler, who added the Later-Gothic touches in the choir vault, the nave and tower. Various events delayed construction: the Hussite wars, a fire in the 15th century, pillage in the 17th... In fact the cathedral was not completed until 1929!

The present entrance under the western, neo-Gothic façade dates from this century. For 500 years, the main entrance was through the Golden Portal on the southern façade. The vaulted roof, supported by 28 pillars, covers three naves 125 m (410 ft) long, 60 m (200 ft) wide and more than 34 m (100 ft) high. Not far from the entrance, on the left, a large stained-glass window designed by Alfons Mucha illustrates the legend of St Methodius. Further on, to the right, the Chapel of St Wenceslas is venerated by the people of Prague. This 14th-century Gothic masterpiece was built on the site where Wenceslas, patron saint of

Bohemia, was buried. In the chapel, the statue of the saint bearing a lance dates from 1373. The walls are decorated with 1,345 precious stones. The murals, from the beginning of the 16th century, illustrate the story of St Wenceslas. Pursued by his brother Boleslav, he managed to grasp the bronze lion's-head doorknocker as he sought sanctuary, but did not make it inside, and was slain by his brother's sword.

A stairway leads to the Royal Treasury, locked in by no less than seven keys. The crown jewels of Bohemia are kept here, including a sword, the crown, sceptre, orb, mantle and stoles.

As you look around the cathedral, notice St John Nepomuk's extravagant tomb, fashioned in 1733–36 from two tonnes of silver. The cathedral pulpit is in Renaissance style. In front of the neo-Gothic high altar, an imposing mausoleum contains the remains of Emperor Ferdinand I of Habsburg, his wife, and their son Maximilian. From the Chapel of the Holy Cross, a stairway leads to the royal crypt containing the tombs of Charles IV, his four wives, and their children. The Chapel of Saxony and Chapel of Our Lady, containing Gothic tombs, are closer to the choir.

Climb the stairs to the top of the

cathedral tower. It's hard going, but well worth the effort for the sweeping view of Prague.

Once outside the cathedral, turn to the right to admire the Golden Portal, crowned by a superb 14th-century mosaic and decorated with figures of the kings of Bohemia and of Charles IV and his wife.

A bit further on, you reach the Mihulka Powder Tower where Rudolf II's alchemists used to carry out their experiments (visit the exhibition).

Old Royal Palace
: Starý Královský palác

This building, located at the further end of the Third Courtyard, was the residence of the Bohemian princes up to the 16th century. The magnificent Vladislav Hall was begun in 1493 by Benedikt Ried, who was knighted for the achievement. With a length of 62 m (200 ft), it is the largest vaulted hall of Europe in Flamboyant Gothic style. Jousting tournaments and banquets were once held here, and the staircase you take was originally designed for horses. Nowadays, the presidential elections are monitored here.

From Vladislav Hall, you can reach the Renaissance-style Louis Palace, named after Louis Jaguellon, son of Vladislav, on the right, then, to the left, the old Diet Hall where the kings were elected.

Today, newly elected presidents take the oath here, as prescribed in the Constitution.

To terminate your visit, see the Chapel of All Saints.

St George's Basilica
: Basilika sv. Jiří

The square behind the cathedral was the castle's central square in the Middle Ages. Facing you is the baroque façade of the basilica, topped by a statue of St George. The interior of the church, with three naves and two towers, is Romanesque. Don't miss the beautiful 12th-century paintings and various tombs.

St George's Convent
: Klášter sv. Jiří
: Open daily except Monday,
: 10 a.m.–6 p.m.

Adjoining the basilica, the convent of the same name, founded in 973, is believed to be the oldest building in Bohemia. It houses 14th–18th-century collections of Gothic, Renaissance and baroque paintings and sculptures from Bohemia.

Golden Lane
: Zlatá ulička

From St George's Square, take Jiřská Street, then, on the left, the passageway U Daliborky to reach picturesque Golden Lane. Legend relates that Rudolf II installed alchemists' laboratories and workshops here to manufacture gold (thence the name). In fact, this little street was originally inhabited by the gunners of the royal guard. Later, people of modest means found a home here. Franz Kafka's sister lodged at no. 22, and the writer stayed with her for several months.

At either end of the lane, the White Tower and Daliborka Tower form part of the castle fortifications and also served as prisons.

Toy Museum

Muzeum Hraček
Jiřská 6
Open daily except Monday,
9.30 a.m.–5.30 p.m.

If you've brought your children to Prague, take them to see this museum which has an amazing display of toys of every period from antiquity onwards.

Castle Square

Hradčanské náměstí
Fringed with large buildings, this square has at its centre the Plague Column, which commemorates the end of the fearsome epidemic of 1679. At no. 15, a passageway takes you to the Sternberg Palace.

Sternberg Palace

Štenberský palác
Hradčanské náměstí 1
Open daily except Monday
10 a.m.–6 p.m.
Tel. 20 51 45 99

National Gallery collections of European art, with works of the German, Austrian, Dutch and Italian schools, including Dürer, Rembrandt, Rubens, El Greco and Goya.

Military Museum

Vojenské Muzeum
Schwarzenberský palác
Hradčanské náměstí 2
Open daily except Monday
10 a.m.–5 p.m., May to October.

The Schwarzenberg Palace, adorned with remarkable Renaissance sgraffitto work, features a museum of military history which will delight anyone with an interest in collecting toy soldiers.

Loretánské Square

Loretánské náměstí
Going down Loretánská from the top of Castle Square, you reach this square built between 1703 and 1726. At no. 1, the façade of the beer hall U Černého Vola (The Black Ox) features a fresco of St Luke, patron saint of artists, who is shown painting an elegant Madonna and Child. At no. 5, the imposing Černín Palace, the largest

baroque palace in Prague, designed by Italian architects, is today the headquarters of the Ministry of Foreign Affairs. Beyond it you can glimpse the spires of the Loreto church.

Our Lady of Loreto

Loreta
Loretánské náměstí 7
Open daily except Monday,
9 a.m.–12.15 p.m.
and 1–4.30 p.m.

This church was built between 1626 and 1750 in honour of Loreto, a well-known place of pilgrimage in Italy where angels are said to have transported the Casa Santa, the Nazareth house where Jesus and the Virgin Mary once lived.

Try to be there on the hour, when the church's carillon of 27 bells chime a hymn.

Go under the porch to the courtyard where two baroque fountains play, one on each side of a square building which is the sculpted and stuccoed replica of the Santa Casa. Inside is a series of paintings relating the life of the Virgin Mary, a silver altar, and a carved wooden Madonna.

The courtyard is surrounded by cloisters on two levels, of which the lower one was reserved for pilgrims. The ground-floor gallery is bordered by 22 altars and 7 chapels. One of these is dedicated to a Spanish saint sporting a beard, which would not seem unusual, except that it happens to be a woman. After begging God to spare her from an arranged marriage, she miraculously sprouted a beard to discourage the suitor.

On the first floor of the cloisters, the Loreto Treasury contains more than 300 religious objects from the 16th to 18th centuries, including candlesticks, chalices and monstrances. The most remarkable exhibit is a diamond-studded monstrance made in Vienna in the 17th century: 89.5 cm (35 in) high and weighing 12 kilos (26 lb), it represents a sun with rays fashioned out of 6,200 diamonds. Everything is well labeled in English as well as Czech.

End your tour by visiting the Nativity Church, built between 1734 and 1737, to admire the striking fresco on the ceiling, depicting the presentation of Jesus in the Temple.

Nový Svět Street

This is probably one of the most picturesque walks to be enjoyed in Prague. If you need a bit of peace after a tiring visit to the castle, it provides a welcome change of scenery.

From the Loreto, take the steep, cobbled Černínská Street on the right, passing gardens and sleepy villas. Then turn right into peaceful Nový Svět, a narrow, winding street that takes you past an excellent restaurant, U Zlaté Hrušk, at no. 3. Turn right again on Kanovnická to return to the Castle Square.

Strahov Monastery

- Strahovský klášter
- Strahovské nádvoří 1/132
- Open daily except Monday
- 9 a.m.–noon, 1.30–5 p.m.

Walk due west of the Loreto to Pohořelec Square. From no. 8, a narrow stairway climbs to the courtyard of the superb Strahov monastery. The main entrance is a bit further up.

Established in 1143 by the Order of Premonstratensians, the monastery was transformed into a museum in 1952, but it was returned to the monks only a few years ago. Apart from the attractive façades of the churches of St Roch and Our Lady, the monastery is especially known for its splendid 12th-century library, made up of more than 130,000 books, 25,000 manuscripts and 2,000 incunabula. The Theological Hall is redolent of history and erudition. It was designed by an Italian architect in 1671 especially to store religious books. On the ceiling, frescoes painted by one of the monks in 1727 are a symbolic celebration of books. Notice the globes showing the world as it was known in the 17th century. The 32-m (144-ft) Philosophical Hall contains more than 50,000 works on philosophy and history, beneath a ceiling fresco illustrating the story of mankind.

Beyond the monastery courtyard, you can enjoy a fantastic view over the city of Prague, with the castle to the left and Malá Strana spreading below. Úvoz Street takes you back to Malá Strana.

Petřín Hill Observation Tower

- Petřínská Rozhledna
- Open daily 9.30 a.m.–6 p.m. April, May and October;
- 9.30 a.m.–8 p.m. June–Sept.;
- 9.30 a.m.–5 p.m. weekends only November–March.

Behind the entrance to the Strahov monastery, a winding path through wooded groves on Petřín hill leads to the 60-m (200-ft) Observation Tower, a replica of the Eiffel Tower erected in 1891 as part of an exhibition. For a wide-angle view of Prague, climb the 299 steps to the top of the tower. Be warned: the tower has the unnerving habit of swaying slightly in a strong wind. From Petřín, you can return to Malá Strana by cable car, which operates 9.15 a.m.–8.45 p.m.

OTHER MONUMENTS

Vyšehrad Castle

- Praha 2
- Soběslavova 1
- By metro, Line C, Vyšehradská station

According to old Czech legends, the first princes of Bohemia dwelt here on top of a rocky outcrop. In the 11th century, Prince Vratislav II built a Romanesque palace and several churches. Later, Emperor Charles IV contributed a royal palace. Vyšehrad eventually developed into a fortress, which was finally destroyed in 1866. Head for St Martin's rotunda, which dates from the 11th century and is the oldest part of Vyšehrad. Originally Romanesque, the Basilica of Sts Peter and Paul was reconstructed in Gothic style during Emperor Charles IV's reign.

Many illustrious personages lie in the Vyšehrad cemetery, among them the composers Smetana and Dvořák, writers Jan Neruda and Karel Čapek, and artists Mikoláš Aleš and Alfons Mucha.

Mozart House

- Praha 5
- Smíchov, Mozartova 169
- Metro Line B, Anděl station
- Open daily except Tuesday
- 10 a.m.–5 p.m.

The elegant Villa Bertramka, located some distance from the centre of Prague, was the home of Czech composer and pianist František Xaver Dušek and his wife, Josefína. Mozart was a frequent guest and it was here, in 1787, that he composed the opera, *Don Giovanni*. Nowadays, musical evenings are organized at Villa Bertramka. There's also a museum devoted to Mozart, containing his white harpsichord and a grand piano.

Dvořák Museum

- Dvořákovo Muzeum
- Ke Karlovu 20
- Metro Line C, IP station
- Open daily except Monday, 10 a.m.–5 p.m.

The museum devoted to composer Dvořák is situated in the little red palace, better known as Villa Amerika, that once belonged to a nobleman, Michna of Vacino. It was built at the beginning of the 18th century by the brilliant architect Kilián Ignác Dienzenhofer, in baroque style. The museum displays Dvořák's original scores, his quill, letters, photographs and personal belongings, including the cap and gown he wore when he received an honorary doctorate from Cambridge University in 1891. Musical recitals are staged here in an intimate atmosphere.

Entertainment

As evening falls, the street lamps fill Prague with a warm, golden light, conducive to mystery and poetry. The palaces of Malá Strana, the baroque churches, the theatres and the concert halls come alive with music and song. The Czechs love dressing up to go to a concert or show. For a long time, under the communist regime, music was their only means of expressing themselves freely.

Programmes for the various performances are distributed in the streets some hours in advance. Concerts and operas usually start around 7 p.m.

THEATRE

In Prague, three great theatres stand out especially for their superb architecture, which puts the audience in a suitably festive mood even before the curtain rises.

National Theatre

Národní divadlo
Národní 2
Tel. 24 91 34 37
At the northern end of Wenceslas Square, turn right along 28. října

Street and on to Národní. Opera, ballet and plays are staged here.

State Opera

- Státní Opera Praha
- Wilsonova 4
- Tel. 24 22 76 93

Estates Theatre

- Stavovské divadlo
- Ovocný trh 1
- Tel. 24 21 50 01

OTHER VENUES

Rodolphinum

- Náměstí Jana Palacha 1

A neo-Renaissance building constructed between 1876 and 1884, headquarters of the Czech Philarmonic Orchestra. The Dvořák hall is famous for its concerts staged during the Prague Spring music festival.

Ahasver – Legends of Magic Prague

- Lucerna Hall, Štěpánská 61
- Tel. 57 92 18 35

A fantastic show on the mysteries of Prague. The actors' skill is enhanced by amazing special effects. Book.

The St Michael Mystery

- Michalská 27–29

St Michael's Church is the setting of a themed attraction described as "a Kafka-esque experience": a walking tour through Czech history, culminating in the Velvet Revolution.

Laterna Magika

- Nová Scéna National Theatre
- Národní 4
- Tel. 24 91 41 29

A unique display combining theatre and cinema will enchant you with its poetry.

National Marionette Theatre

- Žatecká 1
- Old Town
- Tickets and information daily
- 10 a.m.–8 p.m.

Tel. 232 34 29, 232 25 36,
232 41 89

Behind the curtain and the colourful stage sets, the puppeteers wielding the wooden characters are professional actors. The tradition dates back to the 17th century: when German was imposed as the official language, puppets were allowed to continue "speaking" Czech—a valuable way of preserving local culture. The performance of *Don Giovanni* is a saucy look at Mozart's opera.

Bertramka – Muzeum W.A. Mozart

"Original Music Theatre Prague" Villa Bertramka, Mozartova 169 Praha 5
Tel. 54 38 93; 54 00 12

Mozart met with considerable success in Prague, a refreshing change from the mockery he had to endure in Salzburg, his home town. When he conducted the premiere of *Don Giovanni* in the Estates Theatre in 1787, Mozart was the guest of Dušeks, who provided these bucolic surroundings where he could compose in peace. Today, musical evenings (champagne included) are organized in the villa, some distance from the centre of Prague. Mozart's works are performed by actors and singers in superb period costumes.

CLUBS

A trendy atmosphere prevails in the following nightspots:

Malostranská beseda

Malostranské náměstí 21
Open 11 a.m.–10 p.m.
Tel. 53 55 28

On the first floor of the old Malá Strana town hall. In the evening, jazz, folk, country and rock groups perform in the small hall patronized by those in the know. Informal ambience.

Radost FX

Bělehradská 120
Open 9 p.m.–5 a.m.
Tel. 24 25 47 76

This place is divided into several areas so you can move around and enjoy yourself well into the small hours. You can dine, or just have a coffee or a drink. Dancefloor in the basement, with techno music.

Reduta

Národní 20
Tel. 24 91 22 46

For jazz lovers.

Jazz Club Železná

Železná 16
Open 3 p.m.–midnight
Tel. 24 21 25 41

Laid-back atmosphere, very popular with the locals.

Dining Out

The expansive girth of many Prague citizens is ample proof of the richness of the local cuisine: heavy sauces, calorie-loaded pastries, plenty of beer... You may as well put your diet on hold while you're in Prague. If you don't want to spend too much, get away from the city centre and dine in one of the smaller restaurants, often serving good food in copious helpings. In the more touristy areas the bill can be much higher, but prices still compare well with those practised in other European capitals. It must be admitted that occasionally the welcome, service and courtesy in Prague restaurants leave something to be desired.

BEER HALLS

If beer is your tipple you would be well advised to venture into a pivnice (beer hall). There's plenty going on in these noisy, smoke-filled establishments, and the sight of the waiters laden with overflowing jars, nimbly dancing from one table to the other, is fascinating.

If you ask for a *pivo* you will be served half a litre, around a pint. If that seems a bit excessive, try a *malé pivo* (small beer), about a third of a litre, just over half a pint.

The Czechs have an infallible method for testing their beer for quality: if you place a 10-halířů coin on the foam, you should be able to count to ten before it sinks.

U Fleků
⋮ Křemencova 11
⋮ New Town
⋮ Tel. 24 91 51 18

A venerable beer hall, which has been serving a dark beer since 1499. It has six 16th-century

---

THE BEST BEER

Beer is the Czech national drink. The secret of its flavour lies in the quality of the hops, grown in northern Bohemia, and of the water and malt used. According to the ancient chronicles, hops were grown in Bohemia back in the 9th century. The beer trade was considered so important that the king of Bohemia himself granted the licence for brewing it. In the 16th century, beer was spiced up with nutmeg, bay and juniper berries.

Among the various types of beer on offer today, try the light Staropramen or Gambrinus (a Pilsener), both appreciated for their bitter taste. Budvar is somewhat milder. *Světlé pivo* is light beer, and *černé pivo* is dark.

---

vaulted rooms, and quiet gardens for summer drinking. It's quite near the National Theatre, and quite popular with tourists.

Novoměstský Pivovar
⋮ Vodičkova 20
⋮ New Town

The good people of Prague love to meet in the unusual setting of this beer hall, a veritable maze of rooms decorated with old-fashioned murals. You can see the actual brewing vats. It's located on a side street off Wenceslas Square.

U Tomáše
⋮ Letenská 33
⋮ Lesser Quarter

This is the oldest beer hall in Prague, providing liquid refreshment since 1358! There's a fine medieval cellar. A dark beer is brewed on the premises.

CAFÉS

The cafés *(kavárna)* where local intellectuals used to exchange ideas in the early 20th century have almost all disappeared. The legendary Slavia (opposite the National Theatre) has just been opened after seemingly endless years of renovation. You can also sip a Turkish coffee or an expresso at the Savoy, established in 1877. The furniture is a bit too modern, but the ceilings are superb.

Hotel Evropa café

- Václavské náměstí 25
- New Town

The lovely Art Nouveau setting makes a visit to this café worth while, even if the service can be a bit rude. Try a Turkish-style coffee, served in a little silver bowl.

Le Louvre

- Národní 20, New Town
- Open 8 a.m.–11 p.m.

Traditional café decorated with stucco. The clientèle is a strange mix: young people who come to spend hours over their newspapers, and old ladies who meet up for a good gossip.

Kavárna Obecní Dům

- Náměstí Republiky 5, Old Town
- Open 7.30 a.m.–11 p.m.

Located in the Municipal House, next to the Powder Gate. Recently renovated, this is one of the few surviving intellectuals' cafés. The Art Nouveau décor is superb.

Café Milena

- Staroměstské náměstí 22
- Old Town
- Open 10 a.m.–10 p.m.

The café is in the building opposite the astronomical clock, on the first floor. Besides its delicious pastries, the café offers a ring-side seat for observing the activity in the Square.

Molly Malone's Pub

- U Obecního Dvora, Old Town
- Open 11 a.m.–1 a.m.

Believe it or not, Prague has an Irish pub. Thanks to the dusky pink walls, the atmosphere is typically cosy. The floor and chimney piece have been transplanted from an Irish monastery. English-speakers naturally gravitate towards this rustic watering-hole where the tables are old sewing-machine stands. Needless to say, there's Guinness on tap, plus a good selection of Irish whiskey.

RESTAURANTS

Hotel Evropa

- Václavské náměstí 25
- New Town
- Tel. 242 281 17

Sumptuous Art Nouveau decor of stained glass, mahogany, slender caryatids. Good selection of dishes at fairly reasonable prices.

Bellevue

- Smetanovo nábřeží 18
- Old Town
- Open for lunch noon–3 p.m. or dinner 7–11.30 p.m. Brunch-jazz Sundays 11 a.m.–3.30 p.m.
- Tel. 24 22 76 14; fax 24 22 89 32

Excellent cuisine, for example saddle of venison with cranberries and mushrooms. Good view of the castle.

Parnas

Smetanovo nábřeží 2, Old Town
Tel. 24 22 76 14

Excellent cuisine in an appealing Art Nouveau setting. Good view of the castle. Expensive.

Bar-Restaurant La Provence

Štupartská 9, Old Town
Tel. 232 48 01

Very fashionable establishment not far from the Old Town Square. The street-level bar has a fairly flashy atmosphere; for something more refined, go down to the basement dining room for dinner by candle-light.

Francouská Restaurace

Náměstí Republiky, Old Town
Open noon–2.45 p.m. and 6–10 p.m.
Tel. 45 27 20 34

Beautiful establishment recently opened in the enchanting setting of the Municipal House. Interesting French cuisine.

U Zlatých Andělů

Celetná 29, Old Town
Open 10 a.m.–midnight

A good place for meeting Czechs. The atmosphere is informal, and quite boisterous. Good value for money: the food is tasty and helpings generous. Try the goose or the *koleno* (pig's knuckles).

U Prince

Staroměstké náměstí 1
Old Town

Opposite the astronomical clock. Wonderful old-fashioned decor in vaulted dining rooms, and extremely good cuisine. Try the venison salad with olives, the Parma ham with horseradish, or the grilled duck. Reasonable prices.

Chez Marcel

Haštalské náměstí 12
Old Town
Tel. 231 56 76

The French bistro-style decor of this restaurant is reasonably authentic, and the steaks are thick, tender and delicious.

U Zlatého Tygra

Husova 17
Old Town

This is a typical Czech tavern, between the Old Town Square and Charles Bridge. The prices are very reasonable. Very few tourists ever venture into this establishment, which is another rendez-vous of Prague's intellectuals. Highbrow and smoky atmosphere guaranteed. The vaulted room dates from the 13th century.

Try the strong-smelling "beer cheese", which resembles the pungent Alsatian Munster cheese. It is served with bread.

U Zlatého Stromu
- Karlova 6

Near Charles Bridge. The dining room of "The Golden Tree" dates back to the first half of the 13th century. The food is particularly tasty, and, a great help, the menu is printed in several languages.

Kampa Park
- Na Kampě 8b
- Lesser Quarter

- Open 11.30 a.m. to 1 a.m.
- Tel. 57 31 34 93

Romantic setting under Charles Bridge. Pretty terrace in summer. Try the catfish.

U Staleté Báby
- Na Kampě 14
- Lesser Quarter
- Open noon to midnight

Relaxing and intimate setting. Good selection of fish.

THE TASTE OF PRAGUE

Czech delis always take the first-time visitor by surprise. They are veritable monuments to the glory of the pig: festooned in sausages and saveloys, bolonies, hams and various other cooked meats. The smell can be over-powering. There's no doubt that in Prague the sausage is king.

Apart from the traditional grilled sausages served with mild mustard on a slice of bread at the stands on Wenceslas Square, there are other specialities worth seeking out when you want more than a snack. When you decipher the restaurant menus, you'll see *pečená kachna* (grilled duck) or *husa* (goose). There's also venison with cranberries and cream *(srnčí)* and pork, smoked or otherwise, often in breadcrumbs and fried *(smažený řízek)*. Hearty eaters might like to tackle *koleno* (pig's knuckles) served with mild mustard or black radish. Vegetarians are in trouble, but they can always fall back on fish or *smažený sýr* (deep-fried cheese).

It isn't worth ordering several courses; this is not dainty nouvelle cuisine. Usually, a serving fills up the whole plate. Pork is often accompanied by a generous helping of sweetish sauerkraut, with the inevitable bread dumplings called *knedlíky.* You could do worse than order the carp in bread-crumbs *(kapr)*, a traditional Christmas dish.

If you have a sweet tooth you'll be spoiled for choice. The *zákusky* (cream cakes) are irresistible, as are the *palačinky*, pancakes filled with whipped cream, fruit and ice cream, sometimes flambéed. Another tempting possibility is the classic *štrůdl.*

As they say in Prague, *Dobrou chut'*—enjoy your meal!

Moravská Vinárna
- Lesser Quarter
- Closed in winter.

A little open-air restaurant beneath one of the arches of Charles Bridge, on an arm of the Vltava river. Beer and Moravian white wine is served with homely dishes you may have forgotten such as brawn.

U Malířů
- Maltézské náměstí 11
- Lesser Quarter
- Tel. 57 32 03 17

This is arguably the best restaurant in Prague, offering French cuisine. The setting is charming, all velvet and old murals and subdued lighting. Restricted number of tables. The menu is impressive—quail in Armagnac, foie gras, lobster—with prices to match.

Černý Orel
- U Lužického Semináře 40
- Lesser Quarter

At the sign of the Black Eagle, a small, friendly restaurant in a rustic setting, serves good home cooking such as spinach omelette, oven-baked smoked pork, goose, knedliky dumplings with bacon and sauerkraut.

Palffy Palác
- Valdštejnské 14
- Lesser Quarter

- Open 11 a.m.–11 p.m.
- Tel. and fax 57 32 05 70

On the first floor of a magnificent 18th-century palace, this restaurant looks out over gardens that have been recently restored. You can dine on the terrace in summer. This is one of the best addresses in Prague; excellent scallops.

U Zlaté Hrušky
- Nový svět 3
- Castle district
- Tel. 205 15 356

Medieval décor and excellent cuisine, but fairly expensive. Let yourself be tempted by the delicious duck with honey and almonds. Reservations advisable.

Vikárka
- Vikárská 39
- Castle district
- Tel. 55 51 58

Fairly good restaurant behind St Vitus's Cathedral, where you can rub shoulders with Czech ministers.

Hanavský Pavilon
- Letenské sady 173
- Castle district
- Tel. 32 57 92

This little baroque palace is located in the city heights, affording a superb view of the Old Town and the bridges over the Vltava. Reservations essential.

Shopping

Apart from shops specializing in glittering crystal and appealing souvenirs, Prague has several attractive fashion boutiques, some of them housed in palaces, and there are plenty of antique shops, where prices tend to be high.

In general, shops are open Monday to Friday 9 a.m. to 6 p.m., and some close an hour for lunch. The larger stores stay open until 8 p.m.

FOOD

Supermarkets in the centre of Prague are as well stocked as those of other European cities, with a wide range of products. If you need a few picnic items, you can go to one of the many neighbourhood *potraviny* (grocery shops). For the sweet-toothed, there are plenty of *cukrárna* (pastry shops).

Krone

Václavské náměstí 21
Open Monday–Saturday
9 a.m.–8 p.m.,
Sunday 9 a.m.–7 p.m.
This is a large supermarket handily located near the Můstek metro station, at the Václavské náměstí exit.

Pronto Supermarket

- 28. října 9
- Open Monday–Friday
- 7 a.m.–8 p.m.,
- Saturday 7 a.m.–2 p.m.

Supermarket with numerous extra services such as quick shoe repairs.

Dům Lahůdek

- Malé náměstí 3
- Open Monday–Saturday
- 10 a.m.–8 p.m.,
- Sunday 1 p.m.–8 p.m.

The most elegant gourmet grocery in Prague, in a splendid house of Romanesque origin whose façade was decorated by the famous Mikoláš Aleš. Quality teas, cakes, chocolates, spirits and a well-stocked winecellar make this store well worth a visit.

FASHION AND ACCESSORIES

Top boutiques and stores, many of them with a futuristic design, are on a par with the best in Europe. Well-known brands in fashion, perfumes, shoes and so on are available.

Pasáž Myslbek – Nákupní Gallery

- Na Příkopě 19/21

Shopping centre located at the bottom of Wenceslas Square. The boutiques are all new.

Darex

- Václavské námesti 11
- Open 9 a.m.–8 p.m.

Shopping centre.

Model

- Václavské námestí 28
- Open Monday–Friday
- 9 a.m.–7 p.m.;
- Saturday 10 a.m.–5 p.m.

If you suddenly find you need a new hat, call in here. Attractive designs, and prices so reasonable you might as well buy two.

Vinohoradský Pavilon

- Vinohradská 50
- Open Monday–Saturday
- 9.30 a.m.–9 p.m.,
- Sunday noon to 6 p.m.

This could well be the best shopping centre in Prague. In the basement there's a branch of the Pronto supermarket, open from Monday to Saturday from 8 a.m.–9 p.m. and Sunday from noon until 6 p.m.

GIFTS

Prague isn't the ideal place for buying antiques as prices in the city centre are prohibitive. Furthermore, you need special permission to take antiques out of the country; export of religious objects is forbidden. If you want to buy presents for your friends at home, you could settle on a bottle or two of Becherovka liqueur, which tastes a bit like Chartreuse, or you could consider crystal or puppets.

Moser
- Na Příkopě 12
- Open Monday–Friday
- 9 a.m.–7 p.m., Saturday to 4 p.m.,
- Sunday 10 a.m.–4 p.m.
- Tel. 24 21 12 93

A good address for Moser crystal, in a fairytale setting. It's very fragile but refined and superbly crafted.

Sklo Bohemia
- Na Příkopě 17
- Open Monday–Saturday
- 9 a.m.– 7.30 p.m.
- Tel. 24 21 05 74

A huge range of Bohemia brand glass, cut, etched and coloured. The lead content contributes to solidity.

Český Národní Podnik
- Melantrichova 17
- Karlova 12
- Nerudova 31

These shops in the city centre offer handcrafted wood items, decorated Easter eggs and so on.

Kotva
- Náměstí Republiky 8

A sort of Selfridges, Czech style, with several floors. You'll find just about everything here; crystal is a good buy.

Antikvariát U Karlova Mostu
- Karlova 2
- Tel. 26 21 86

A musty smell beckons lovers of old books.

Alma starozitnosti
- Valentinska 7

This antique shop in the Old Town has a treasure-trove of 1920s to 1940s costume jewellery in the basement, much of it retrieved from Bohemian factories closed during communist rule.

PUPPETS

The Czechs have been very fond of puppets since the days when German was imposed as the official language, and only marionettes had the right to express themselves in Czech. Today, string, glove and rod puppets are sold in countless shops and stalls in the centre of Prague. Before you buy, compare prices and the materials used: wood, plaster, china. Among the characters dearest to the Czechs are Kašpárek, an amiable clown dressed in red, and Honza, the simple country lad who, thanks to his common sense, saved a princess from being devoured by a dragon and ended up by marrying her. Not forgetting the Good Soldier Švejk with his cap and somewhat naive expression.

Excursions

The Czech Republic is made up of two regions—Bohemia in the west and Moravia in the east. It is said to be the European country with the largest number of castles per inhabitant. Take time to explore the countryside, away from the main roads and the big cities. Travelling through dense forests of fir trees, you will suddenly stumble upon a fortress, a Renaissance castle or the colourful main square in a small provincial town.

BOHEMIA

If all that hearty Czech food is proving to be more than your system can take, a stay in one of the spa towns, Karlovy Vary, Marienbad or Františkovy Lázně, may be just what the doctor ordered. All three boast a privileged setting for hydrotherapy cures.

These towns used to be a favourite gathering place for the aristocracy. Later they were popular with *maminkas* (as the Czechs affectionately call their mums), who could enjoy cures free of charge under the communist regime. After the Velvet Revolution, the spa buildings were restored to offer once again the healthy benefits of natural springs in a refined environment.

Many famous people have frequented these havens of peace: Bismarck, Brahms, Chopin, Chateaubriand, Freud, Marx, Tolstoy and more. One of the most loyal clients was Goethe, a great believer in hydrotherapy, who met here the last great love of his life, Ulrike von Levetzov, 55 years his junior.

Karlovy Vary

Karlovy Vary, 118 km (73 miles) from Prague, is very popular with German visitors seeking relief from their ailments. The stylized buildings date from the 17th, 18th and 19th centuries. The thermal springs, approved in 1358 by Charles IV, total a dozen and their waters are endowed with medicinal qualities for treating back pains, obesity, and high blood pressure.

Few pleasures can beat a stroll through the landscaped gardens, beneath the Mill Colonnade, an elegant neoclassical construction, or the more modern Spring Colonnade, where the healing waters gush forth. Regular concerts are held to cheer up the water-drinkers, who are all equipped with a *kalíšek*, a spouted porcelain cup (you can buy one if you want).

The town of Karlovy Vary stands on several hills in the middle of a forest. You can visit the splendid Russian Orthodox church, the Grand Hotel Pupp and the Baths where you can soak in the same tub as the illustrious emperor Francis Joseph. High above the town, hidden among the firs, the Imperial Hotel looks like an impregnable citadel. The Soviet leaders used to gather here for opulent partying; Brezhnev had his own suite.

Mariánské Lázně

Verdant Marienbad looks as if it were built on a golf course. The architecture is similar to that of Karlovy Vary, including an elegant colonnade built in 1889, next to the more modern "singing" fountain.

Františkovy Lázně

Founded in 1791, this is a true haven of peace, with 25 thermal springs, well-maintained parks and gardens, and bandstands.

Cheb

Not far from Františkovy Lázně, on the border with Bavaria, the little town of Cheb takes you into the past, with its medieval marketplace and town hall, its 13th-century timber-frame houses that belonged to Jewish merchants, its Gothic churches and its castle.

Tábor

Tábor, 88 km (55 miles) south of Prague, was built as a fortress by Jan Žižka, a Hussite commander, with the streets laid out in a maze to confuse invaders. The religious and political movement split into two factions in the 15th century, and Tábor was the headquarters of the more militant Taborite group. The museum in the Gothic town hall is devoted to the Hussite movement. The Transfiguration Church, the Augustinian church and the Kotnov castle are also of architectural interest.

Jindřichův Hradec

South of Tábor, Jindřichův Hradec has a lovely triangular square bordered by Renaissance, baroque and classical buildings. A quick tour of the town should include the Trinity column (1764), the castle at the edge of the carp-filled pond, and the old beer hall.

Červená Lhota

Between Tábor and Jindřichův Hradec, the castle of Červená Lhota is a Renaissance manor surrounded by a pond which mirrors the castle's bright red walls, a delightful sight.

České Budějovice

The arcaded square of this city of 95,000 is said to be the largest in Bohemia. Each side measures 130 m (425 ft), utterly charming and harmonious, bordered by Gothic, baroque and Renaissance buildings and listed as a historical monument. You can tour the square in an open carriage.

Hluboká nad Vltavou

With its eleven towers and its bastions standing proudly on a rocky hill, the castle of Hluboká nad Vltavou, 10 km (6 miles) north of Budějovice, seems to have come straight out of a fairy tale. This fortress was built between 1840 and 1881, in the English Windsor style. Worth a visit for its wood panelling, tapestry and the library, holding some 12,000 volumes.

Český Krumlov

Further south, the town of Český Krumlov, founded in the 12th century, nestles on the banks of the Vltava river. There are 250 monuments of interest here. The castle, the second-largest in the country after Prague's, dates back to the 13th century. It was later adapted to the Renaissance style. Visit the hall of masks and the baroque theatre.

Karlštejn Castle

Surrounded by forested hills, this castle 28 km (17 miles) south of

Prague is the work of the French architect Matthias of Arras at the request of Charles IV, built 1348–57. Its purpose was to store the royal and imperial crown jewels. The latter were moved to Prague Castle in 1625. The exhibition in the Courtesans Hall traces the history of Karlštejn, while the Luxembourg Hall features the busts of Charles IV's family. Do not miss the Chapel of St Catherine, the walls of which are covered in precious stones.

Konopiště

The castle of Konopiště, 40 km (25 miles) southeast of Prague, was built in the 12th century, and then rebuilt in the late-Gothic style, with further Renaissance additions. It is famous for its large park and the arms and armour collection of the Austrian Archduke Franz Ferdinand, who was a passionate hunter and would shoot anything with fur or feathers. His murder in Sarajevo in 1914 sparked off World War I.

Kutná Hora

This medieval town 65 km (40 miles) southeast of Prague is famous for its silver mines, which operated between the 12th and 18th centuries. Through the courtyard of the Vlašský dvůr (Italian Court), you reach the museum which includes the workshops where coins were minted. The superb Gothic Cathedral of St Barbara, the patron saint of miners, is one of the most outstanding in Bohemia. Begun in 1388 to plans by Peter Parler, the project was later completed by Benedikt Rieth and Matthias Rejsek. The macabre Sedlec Chapel, 3 km (2 miles) northwest of the main square, was built in the 12th century and decorated with the bones of 10,000 dead from the adjoining cemetery.

Kuks Castle

Kuks is worth the detour for its open-air museum of baroque art. Having won fame and fortune in the wars, Count Franz Anton Špork commissioned an Italian architect to design an original setting in which to entertain his glittering court. Built between 1694 and 1724, Kuks was a combination of castle and spa town. All you can visit from this dazzling period are the hospice and the fabulous Pharmacy Hall. But it is worth coming just to see the statues sculpted by Matyáš Bernhard Braun. Standing in front of the castle as if they were gazing across the countryside, they represent, with uncanny expressiveness, human vice and virtue.

MORAVIA

Moravia is known for its folklore, its traditions and the sweetness of its wines (especially in the south).

Brno

Brno, 196 km (120 miles) southeast of Prague, is the unofficial capital of Moravia. It's the country's second-largest city with around 390,000 inhabitants, and welcomes trade fairs and conventions all year long. Among the famous people who lived in Brno are the geneticist Grégor Mendel, the composer Leoš Janáček and the writer Milan Kundera. Archaeological excavation has revealed that Brno has its roots in prehistoric times. It was a trading village that achieved the status of town in 1243. Enclosed within ramparts in the Middle Ages, it developed into a significant settlement in the 14th century. You can visit the castle on Špilberk hill, which first served as the residence of the Moravian princes in the 13th century, and then became a fortress under the Habsburgs. The Gothic Cathedral of Sts Peter and Paul, with its two finely sculpted spires, is visible from afar. Construction began in 1140 and took 30 years to complete. Refurbished in baroque style in the 18th century, the cathedral is daunting in size: the nave measures 64 m (210 ft). The 16th-century pulpit and a14th-century sandstone statue of the Madonna are particularly remarkable.

In the centre of Brno, the marketplace is known for its baroque Parnas Fountain, designed by the architect Johann B. Fischer von Erlach. It depicts Hercules chaining up Cerberus. The Dietrichstein Palace, housing the Museum of Moravia, dominates the square. At no. 4 is the Reduta Theatre where Mozart performed in 1767. You can also visit the former town hall and climb to the top of its tower.

For a more gruesome visit, see the Capuchin Convent (Kapucínský klášter, Kapucínské náměstí 5), which contains mummies of monks and various illustrious personages such as Baron Trench, who battled against the Turks in the 18th century. Until Emperor Joseph II banned the practice in 1784, the dead were set out to dry and mummify in the sun.

The crypt is open Tuesday to Saturday, 9 a.m. to noon and 2 to 4.30 p.m., Sundays 11–11.45 a.m. and 2–4 p.m.

Watched over by its Gothic cathedral, Brno is the Czech Republic's second-largest city.

Slavkov (Austerlitz)

The monument dedicated to peace at Slavkov, also known as Austerlitz, 20 km (12 miles) east of Brno, was raised to commemorate the battle waged by Napoleon on December 2, 1805, when he defeated an army of 90,000 Russian and Austrian troops. Every year, the battle is re-enacted at the site. In Slavkov, the baroque castle houses an exhibition dedicated to the life of Napoleon.

Strážnice

South of Brno, they treat wine and folklore in the same manner: with lots of enthusiasm. In Strážnice, to the southeast, grannies ride around on bicycles, dressed in traditional garb, their skirts billowing in the wind. A large open-air museum recalls village life in times gone by. At the end of June the biggest folklore festival in the country is held here.

Mikulov

Near the border with Austria, Mikulov (to the south) is a charming wine-growing town with an imposing baroque castle and an old central square. In summer, very colourful folklore festivals are held here, when whole pigs are barbecued in the town hall courtyard.

Telč

One of the country's gems, this town has been designated as a world heritage site by UNESCO, for its castle and its elongated market square, its gabled houses, Renaissance and baroque façades and arcades. The houses bordering the central square all look alike. One large hall called *mazhaus* served for trade or selling beer. Notice, at no. 15, the pretty corbel construction, with projecting upper floors; at no. 37, the sculpture on the gable end; the baroque façade at no. 59; the sgraffito decoration at no. 61. On the square the "lower" fountain, adorned with the statue of St Margaret, was built in 1611. The other, "upper" fountain, dates from 1827. The castle is rather impressive: see the Renaissance halls with their coffered wood ceilings. Carvings in the Hall of Knights (1570) depict the exploits of Hercules.

Olomouc

This town in northern Moravia was founded in the 11th century. Today it has some 110,000 inhabitants. Take time to stroll in its winding alleys, stopping in the central square, Horní náměstí, to admire the town hall, the astronomical clock, the Trinity Column and the two beautiful baroque fountains.

The Hard Facts

Airport

The Ruzyně International Airport is 15 km (10 miles) from the city centre. You can change money there, and hire a car. There are various means of transport to Prague:

The ČSA minibus runs every 30 minutes from 8.30 a.m. to 7 p.m. Price 95 Kč. It will take you to the Renaissance Hotel, near the Old Town and Na Příkopě.

The Cedaz Express Airport minibus (tel. 20 11 42 96) will take you to the centre, dropping you off at Wenceslas Square, Republic Square or your hotel.

Bus no. 119 takes you to the Dejvická metro station (last station on the A Line).

The privately owned Belinda shuttle company has exclusive rights on transporting airport travellers into (but not out of) the city. The white cars look a bit like taxis but are more expensive.

If you take a real taxi, settle on the fare before you get in (count on a minimum of 350 Kč to the city centre).

City tours

A tour in a horse-drawn carriage is the most romantic way to explore the Old Town, to the sound of hooves clip-clopping on the cobblestones. The pickup point is in the Old Town Square.

In summer, you can take a boat trip on the Vtlava river. Don't forget to take some bread to feed the ducks and swans. Rental of a row boat is 30 Kč per hour. Departure from Slovansky Ostove (Slav Island), under the Legií Bridge, just behind the National Theatre.

Climate

Summers are very hot, and winters bitterly cold, with temperatures sometimes plunging to −20°C (−4°F) in January and February. Snow is not uncommon during these two months. The best time to visit Prague is, of course, spring. Late summer is usually pleasant, and the colours of autumn suit Prague well. The city is less crowded in October and November.

Crime

Increasing numbers of pickpockets in the underground and trams, usually operating in groups, mean you should keep alert while travelling around. You're not likely to find a policeman to help. Keep your money and papers well hidden.

If your credit card is stolen, have it blocked immediately, as

Prague shopkeepers rarely ask for proof of identity.

In case of theft, go to the police station at the bottom of Wenceslas Square (Jungmannovo náměstí 9), where English interpreters will be able to help.

Currency

The Czech monetary unit is the crown (Kč). Coins from 1 to 50 Kč, notes from 20 to 5000 Kč.

Exchange offices in the city centre charge a commission of up to 10%, so you will be better off changing money at a bank, where the charges vary from 2–3%. There are several banks and cash machines on Na Příkopě, and others on Celetná Street. The cashpoint at 33 Na Příkopě (MasterCard, American Express, Visa) operates round the clock, as does the one at the American Express office, 56 Wenceslas Square, open Tuesday to Saturday, 9 a.m.–7 p.m., tel. 24 21 99 78.

Many hotels and restaurants accept payment by credit card.

Driving

When driving, give priority to the right. The speed limits are 110 kph (68 mph) on motorways, 90 kph (55 mph) on national roads and 50 kph (30 mph) in built-up areas. Seatbelts are compulsory, and the consumption of alcohol is strictly forbidden.

If you drive on the motorway you will need to buy a special sticker to display on the windscreen, available in post offices, certain garages, or at the border crossing.

Petrol stations are common along major routes, but less predictable on secondary roads (super petrol is 96 octane).

Car theft is fairly widespread in the country. It is best to park in a surveyed parking lot or the hotel garage.

On the city streets, watch out for the tramways. Their drivers seem to be blissfully unaware of obstacles, be they cars or pedestrians.

Distances:

London 1285 km (788 miles)
Paris 1050 km (652 miles)
Brussels 876 km (544 miles)
Zurich 670 km (416 miles)
Munich 360 km (223 miles)
Brno 98 km (123 miles).

Embassies

Canada
Mickiewiczova 6, 12533 Praha 6
Tel.: 72 10 18 00; fax 72 10 18 90

United Kingdom
Thunovská 14, 118 00 Praha 1
Tel. 57 32 03 55; fax 57 32 10 23

USA
Tržiště 15, 11801 Praha 1
Tel. 57 53 06 63; 57 53 40 28

Emergencies
Medical emergencies: Tel 155
Police: Tel. 158
Fire brigade: Tel 150

Na Homolce Hospital
Roentgenova 2, Praha 5
Tel. 52 92 21 46 Monday to Friday, 8 a.m.–4 p.m. Outside these hours, tel. 57 21 11 11. This hospital, 20 minutes from the city centre, has a good reputation.

The American Medical Center,
tel. 80 77 56, provides reliable medical services by experienced European and American doctors and dentists.

Entry Formalities
European Union, US and Canadian citizens need a valid passport. Australian citizens also need a visa, obtainable from your nearest Czech embassy or consulate. US passport holders need a visa for stays of more than 30 days; holders of New Zealand and Irish passports for stays of more than 90 days, and British and Canadian passport-holders for stays of more than 180 days.

Festivals
The major cultural event of the year is the Prague Spring music festival. Orchestras, ensembles, singing groups and soloists take over the streets and concert halls of the Czech capital.

At Christmas, numerous small outdoor markets set up their stalls in the Old Town. Pride of place is given to an enormous decorated Christmas tree.

Intercity Travel
Trains are slow, and it is best to travel by bus. You can obtain schedules from tourist information offices.

Many buses leave from the Florenc coach terminal. For information—in approximate English—try calling 24 21 10 60, though the line is often busy. The best bet is to go to the terminal in person.

As a guide, the journey from Prague to Brno takes two hours, and the ticket costs 100 Kč. The three-hour trip from Prague to Telč is 80 Kč.

The Florenc coach terminal is open Mon–Fri 6 a.m.–6.30 p.m., Saturday 6 a.m.–1 p.m., Sunday 8 a.m.–3 p.m..

Lost and Found
Karolíny Světlé 5
Tel. 24 23 50 85

Newspapers
Newsagents sell most international titles. For local news, read *The Prague Post* which contains tourist information, cinema and theatre programmes, exhibitions, restaurant listings, etc. It also has a good website:
http://www.praguepost.cz

Opening Hours

Banks open Monday to Friday 8 a.m.–5 p.m.; most shops open 8 or 9 a.m. to 4 or 5 p.m.

Orientation

Above house doors, the number on the blue plate indicates the address while that on the red plate gives the district registration number.

Post

The main post office, open round the clock, is located at Jindřišská 14 (perpendicular to Wenceslas Square). Stamps are sold at counters 10, 11, 14, 15 or 16. To send packets or international parcels, go to counter 17. The poste restante is on the first floor.

The post office in the third courtyard of the Prague Castle opens weekdays 8 a.m.–7 p.m. and weekends 10 a.m.–7 p.m.

Prices

Hotel accommodation is quite expensive, on a par with German prices. Restaurants, on the other hand, are more reasonable.

Public Holidays

January 1	New Year's Day
March/April	Easter Monday
May 1	Labour Day
May 8	Liberation Day
July 5	Feast of Sts Cyril and Methodius
July 6	Commemoration of death of Jan Hus
October 28	Czechoslovak Independence
December 25	Christmas Day

Public Transport

The Prague metro is fast and clean. There are three lines, A (green), B (yellow) and C (red).

You can purchase tickets in newspaper kiosks, underground stations or automatic machines. A 12-Kč ticket is valid for an hour and allows you to change lines. An 8-Kč ticket is valid for a distance of four Metro stations on one line only, or for 15 minutes on the tram. Special tourist passes are available: 70 Kč for 24 hours, 180 Kč for three days, 250 Kč for 7 days, 280 Kč for 15 days.

There's usually a queue in front of the automatic ticket machines, which are slow and impractical. It's best to buy tickets in the newspaper kiosks down the steps in the Můstek and Muzeum Metro stations. Do not forget to stamp your ticket, as inspections are frequent, and you will be fined 200 Kč on the spot if you're thought to be dodging the fare.

Taxis

Prague taxi drivers are notorious for taking tourists for a ride—in more ways than one. The AAA company is considered to be the most professional; tel. 10 80

Before you set off, check the fare, which should be clearly indicated on the front taxi door.

Telephone
Phone booths operate with cards or coins.

The code for the Czech Republic is 420. Area code for Prague is 2, and for Brno, 5.

To make an international call, dial 00 then the country code (1 for Canada and US, 44 for UK) the area code (minus the initial zero) and the local number.

Tipping
In restaurants, it is customary to leave 10% of the bill, even if service has been painfully slow. Pay the tip along with the bill, rather than leaving coins on the table.

Toilets
For the price of a few crowns, you will find clean, attended public toilets down the steps at the Můstek and Muzeum metro stations, at either end of Charles Bridge and in the castle (near the entrance to St Vitus's Cathedral).

Tourist Information
There is a Tourist Information Office in the hall of the main railway station. There are severtal others around town, all pro-

viding information, maps and brochures in English, French and German.

You can also make reservations here for shows, hotels and tour guides.

Old Town Hall
Staroměstská Radnice
Staroměstské náměstí 1
(open 9 a.m.–5.30 p.m.)

Na Příkopě 20
(in the banking street, off the northern end of Wenceslas Square

Prague Tourist Centre
Rytířská 12 (off Wenceslas Square)
Tel. (4202) 24 21 22 09
or 24 23 60 47
Fax. (4202) 24 21 22 09
or 24 23 69 47
The staff in this office are particularly helpful, and receptive to all your problems.

Tours
Numerous travel agencies offer organized tours.

Premiant City Tour, Na Příkopě 23 (tel. 0601 21 26 25) features a boat tour on the Vltava and day trips to the castles of Karlštejn, Kutná Hora, Konopiště and the city of Český Krumlov.

Voltage
Electricity is 220 volts.

Charles Bridge

Strolling along the bridge is like being in a fantastic open-air museum with its thirty statues looming up on each side. We start our walk from the right bank, Old Town end. You'll need a pair of binoculars to study the intricate details.

1
St Yves, protector of the poor and deprived. At his feet, a mother nursing her infant, an old man and a child begging for mercy. M.B. Braun (1711); copy 1908.

2
St Bernard, the Virgin Mary and two cherubs. M.W. Jäckel (1709); copy.

3
St Barbara (centre), St Margaret (left) and St Elizabeth (right). F.M. Brokoff (1707).

4
St Thomas Aquinas (right), the Virgin Mary and St Dominic (left). The dog symbolizes Dominican inquisitors (Domini canes, God's dogs). M.W. Jäckel (1708); copy 1961.

5
Pieta. E. Max (1859).

6
Crucifixion (1629). The Hebrew inscription in golden letters, Holy, Holy, Holy God, was paid for by a Jew accused of blasphemy (1696).

7
St Joseph. E. Max (1854).

8
St Ann. M.W. Jäckel (1707).

9
St Francis Xavier, supported by two converted Moors, an Indian and a Chinese, with a Moorish king awaiting baptism. The kneeling figure represents the sculptor himself, aged 23. F.M. Brokoff (1711); copy 1913.

10
St Cyril and St Methodius, preaching to three disciples. These Byzantine missionaries began christianizing Bohemia and Moravia in 863. K. Dvorák (1938).

11
St Christopher. E. Max (1857).

12
St John the Baptist with his golden cross. J. Max (1857).

13
St Francis Borgia. F.M. Brokoff (1710); restored 1937.

16   14   12   10   8   6   4   2

5   13   11   9   7   5   3   1

Staré Mesto

14

St Norbert flanked by St Wenceslas (left) and St Sergius (right), both clad in armour and carrying a sword. J. Max (1853).

15

St Ludmilla, the grandmother of St Wenceslas (c. 1720).

16

St John Nepomuk with a halo of five golden stars and a crucifix. Touching the bronze plaque is supposed to bring good luck. Canonized in 1729, John Nepomuk was the queen's confessor, thrown into the Vltava at this very spot when he refused to divulge her secrets to Wenceslas IV (1378–1419). J. Brokoff and M. Rauchmüller (1683).

17

St Francis of Assisi and two angels. E. Max (1855).

18

St Anthony of Padua carrying a golden olive branch. J.O. Mayer (1708).

19

St Vincent Ferrer and St Procopius. F.M. Brokoff (1712). Behind is the statue of the knight Bruncvik, standing guard since 1884.

20

St Jude. J.O. Mayer (1708). In summer, the statue is draped in blossom from the trees on Kampa Island down below.

21

St Nicholas of Tolentino carrying a golden olive branch. F. Kohl (1708); copy 1969.

22

St Augustin with his long beard, mitre and golden staff. J.F. Kohl (1708); copy 1974.

23

St Lutgard, a blind Cistercian nun, kneeling before Christ. M.B. Braun (1710).

24

St Cajetan. F.M. Brokoff (1709).

25

St Adalbert, bishop of Prague. F.M. Brokoff (1709).

26

St Philip Benitius. M.B. Mandl (1714).

27

St John of Matha, St Felix of Valois and St Ivan. A king's son, Ivan lived as a hermit in the suburbs of Prague at the end of the 9th century. Here he is collecting money to buy back the Christians held captive by the Turks and guarded by a dog. F.M. Brokoff (1714).

28

St Vitus. F.M. Brokoff (1714).

29

St Wenceslas. J.K. Böhm (1858).

30

St Saviour (centre), St Cosmas (left) and St Damian (right). J.O. Mayer (1709).

The Top Ten

This book aims to guide you to the best monuments, museums, parks, shops, restaurants and cafés in Prague. But where do you start? If you are in a hurry, here's our handy list of the top ten travel tips:

- Admire the Old Town Square and the astronomical clock, pp. 17–19
- Beat the tourist crowds and visit Charles Bridge at sunrise, pp. 24, 60
- Wander around the palaces of the Lesser Quarter, pp. 26–27
- Explore St Nicholas Cathedral in the Lesser Quarter, p. 27
- Take the leafy route to the castle through the Ledebourg Gardens, p. 27
- Travel back in time in the castle's Old Royal Palace, p. 31 and St Vitus's Cathedral, p. 30
- Join the ghosts in a midnight stroll along Nový Svet, p. 33
- Be bewitched by a Laterna Magika show, p. 37
- Sip a coffee in the Art Nouveau setting of the Café Evropa, p. 41
- Dine on roast goose with an excellent lager at a beer hall, pp. 39–40

General editor: Barbara Ender
English adaption: Mark Little
Design: Aude Aquoise
Photos: Renata Holzbachová;
p. 15 Copyright © Mucha Trust 1997
Maps: Elsner & Schichor

Copyright © 2000, 1998 JPM Publications S.A.
12, avenue William-Fraisse, 1006 Lausanne, Suisse
E-mail: information@jpmguides.com
Internet: http://www.jpmguides.com/

Every care has been taken to verify the information in the guide, but the publisher cannot accept responsibility for any errors that may have occurred. If you spot an inaccuracy or a serious omission, please let us know.
Printed in Switzerland — Gessler/Sion

INDEX